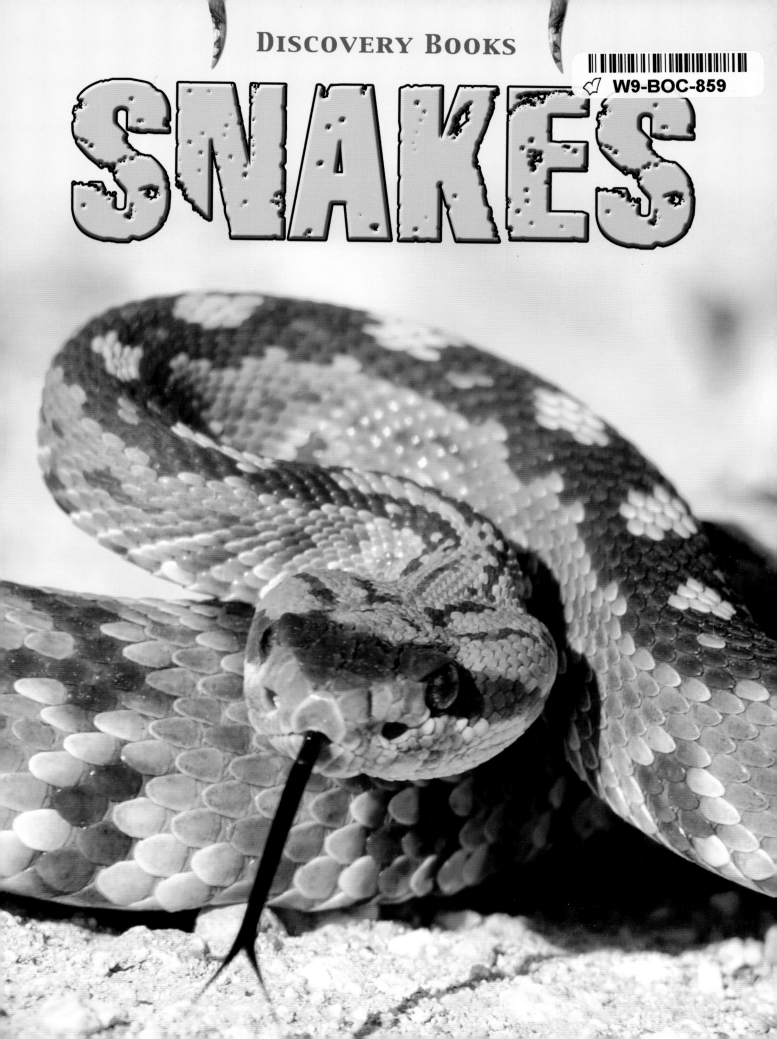

DISCOVERY BOOKS
SNAKES

Q2AMedia

Created by Q2AMedia
www.q2amedia.com
Text, design & illustrations Copyright © Q2AMedia 2012

Scholastic and Tangerine Press and associated logos are
trademarks and/or registered trademarks of Scholastic Inc.

an imprint of
■SCHOLASTIC
www.scholastic.com

Published by Tangerine Press, an imprint of Scholastic Inc.,
557 Broadway; New York, NY 10012

Scholastic Canada Ltd.; Markham, Ontario
Scholastic Australia Pty. Ltd; Gosford NSW
Scholastic New Zealand Ltd.; Greenmount, Auckland

Editor Jessica Cohn
Client Service Manager Ravneet Kaur
Project Manager Arushi Chawla and Shekhar Kapur
Creative Director Joita Das
Designer Cheena Yadav, Deepika Verma, Ravinder Kumar
Picture Researcher Nivisha Sinha

10 9 8 7 6 5 4 3 2 1

ISBN: 978-0-545-35087-7

Printed in Shenzhen, China.

Picture Credits
t= top, b= bottom, c= center, r= right, l= left

Front Cover: Paul S. Wolf/Shutterstock,
Eric Isselee/Shutterstock.

Back Cover: Paytai/Shutterstock.

Title: Jake Holmes/iStockphoto.
Imprint Page: Maria Dryfhout/Shutterstock.
Half Title: Audrey Snider-Bell/Shutterstock.
Contents Page: Rodho/Shutterstock, Eric Isselée/
Shutterstock, Cellistka/Shutterstock.

6t: Rodho/Shutterstock; 6b: Szefei/Shutterstock;
7: Eightofnine; 8t: Paytai/Shutterstock; 8b:
Ingo Arndt/Minden Pictures/National Geographic
Stock; 9: Gordon Galbraith/Shutterstock;
10: Rodho/Shutterstock; 10-11: Four Oaks/
Shutterstock; 11: Chris Alcock/Shutterstock;
12t: David B Fleetham/Oxford Scientific/
Photolibrary; 12b: Bill Love/NHPA; 13t: Maria
Dryfhout/Shutterstock; 13b: Ken Griffiths/
NHPA; 15t: Martin Dohrn/Nature Picture Library;
15b: Tony & Sheila Phelps/Oxford Scientific/
Photolibrary; 16t: Agrosse/Shutterstock;
16b: Kenneth L. Krysko; 17: Birgit Trutnau/
WaterFrame-Underwater Images/Photolibrary;
18t: Scorpp/Shutterstock; 18-19: Travis Houston/
Shutterstock; 20: Borhuah Chen/Shutterstock;
20-21: Malcolm Schuyl/FLPA/Photolibrary; 22t:
Morales/age fotostock/Photolibrary; 22b: John
Cancalosi/Peter Arnold Images/Photolibrary;
23t: Diane White Rosier/iStockphoto; 23b: Rusty
Dodson/Shutterstock; 24t: Chanyut Sribua-rawd/
iStockphoto; 24b: Miroslav Hlavko/Shutterstock;
25: Blaine Harrington/age fotostock/
Photolibrary; 26l: Arztsamui/Shutterstock; 26r:
Tim Laman/National Geographic Stock, Stillfx/
Shutterstock; 27: Dan Exton/Shutterstock;
28: Sergei Chumakov/Shutterstock, Stillfx/
Shutterstock; 29: Amee Cross/Shutterstock; 30:
Fotolia; 31: Bernhard Richter/Shutterstock; 32t:
Mirek Kijewski/Shutterstock; 32b: Photobar/
Shutterstock; 33: Beverly Joubert/National
Geographic Stock; 34-35: Joel Sartore/National
Geographic/Getty Images; 35: Matthijs Kuijpers/
Dreamstime; 36t: Anthony Bannister/NHPA;
36b: Dinodia/age fotostock/Photolibrary;
37t: Ken Griffiths/NHPA; 37b: Digital Vision/
Thinkstock; 38: Chris Mattison/FLPA; 39: Volker
Steger/Science Photo Library/Photolibrary; 40t:
Stephen Mcsweeny/Shutterstock; 40c: Gnilenkov
Aleksey/Shutterstock; 40-41: Maik Dobiey; 41:
Prill Mediendesign & Fotografie/iStockphoto;
42: Tony Phelps/Nature Picture Library; 43t:
Omar Ariff/iStockphoto; 43b: John Cancalosi/
Photolibrary; 44: Fivespots/Shutterstock; 44-45:
Mirosław Kijewski/iStockphoto; 45: Eric Isselée/
Shutterstock; 47: Chris Alcock/Shutterstock; 48:
Omar Ariff/iStockphoto.

Q2AMedia Art Bank: 6, 10, 14, 18-19, 46.

SNAKES

Sally Morgan

Contents

All About Snakes

Snake! The very word sends shivers down the spines of some people. Snakes are like no other animal, with their long, legless bodies and lidless eyes.

Dangerous animals

Most snakes are harmless, but many people fear them because some are incredibly dangerous. Some have **poisonous** bites that can kill a full-grown person in minutes. Millions of people are bitten each year.

◄ The cobra is easily recognized by the distinctive hood.

Sea snakes
Terrestrial snakes

▲ Land snakes, or terrestrial snakes, are found on all continents except Antarctica.

Reptiles

Snakes belong to a group of **vertebrate** animals called **reptiles**. A vertebrate is an animal with a backbone. The backbone runs down the back and supports the body. Reptiles are covered in scaly skin, and most lay eggs. There are many different types of reptiles, including alligators, turtles, and lizards. Snakes and lizards make up more than 90 percent of reptiles.

Snakes are **predators** that hunt other animals. Many snakes produce **venom**, a kind of poison, to kill their prey. Snakes have jaws that unhinge and open wide, so they can swallow prey whole, even large ones.

The smallest snake is *Leptotyphlops carlae*. It lives on the island of Barbados in the Caribbean. It is as thin as spaghetti and about 4 inches (10 centimeters) long.

More Snake Facts

Snakes are cold-blooded animals, but the word *cold-blooded* can be misleading. Many people are surprised when they pick up a snake for the first time. A snake feels warm. A better word to describe these creatures is *ectothermic*, which means "getting heat from the outside." Snakes take heat from the environment to keep their bodies warm.

▲ Many snakes live in trees, where they wait for prey.

The heaviest snake is the anaconda, which weighs 441 pounds (200 kilograms) or more. The longest snake is the reticulated python, which can reach about 33 feet (10 meters) in length.

▼ The anaconda prefers spending time in rivers and swamps. It has a hard time moving on land because of its size.

Living with dinosaurs

Snakes and lizards have lived on Earth for millions of years. They were around at the same time as the **dinosaurs**. One type of snake, called *Sanajeh indicus*, was one of the few animals known to prey on dinosaurs. It lived 67 million years ago. This creature waited close to dinosaur nests and attacked the hatchlings as they emerged from the eggs.

Snake god

The Aztecs and Mayans of Central America worshipped a snake god named Quetzalcoatl (ket-sahl-kah-WAH-tel). This name means "feathered serpent." The feathers were like those of a brightly colored bird named the quetzal. Quetzalcoatl was splendid in appearance, but deadly, too. People believed that this god could fly and give life. Quetzalcoatl also represented rebirth, because snakes can shed their skin to reveal new skin underneath. Many of the temples of the region have carvings of feathered snakes.

The Snake Family

There are almost 3,000 different **species**, or types, of snakes in the world. They are divided into different groups according to their features. The main types of snakes are the boas and pythons, colubrids, elapids, and vipers.

▲ *The lips of boas and pythons are lined with heat sensors, which help them find prey.*

Boas and pythons

This snake family contains six of the world's largest snakes, including the anaconda and reticulated python. These snakes are all constrictors. They wrap themselves around their prey to **suffocate** it. Anacondas are so heavy that they live much of their lives in or near water. The water supports their weighty bodies. Many boas live in trees. They have a **prehensile** (pree-HEN-sahl) tail that acts a bit like a limb, wrapping itself around objects and gripping firmly.

Colubrids

Two-thirds of all snakes belong to this group. That's about 1,600 species. Colubrids include common snakes, such as the corn and garter snakes. This group is so large, it's not surprising that the snakes are varied in their size and appearance. Some of the snakes in this group are small, such as the thin racers that actively hunt small prey. The larger species, such as the grass snake, reach several feet (meters) in length. This group used to be considered harmless, but there are some venomous members, such as the boomslang, an African tree snake.

▼ The venomous boomslang has an egg-shaped head and large eyes.

The skin of a boomslang is one of the ingredients of Polyjuice Potion in the Harry Potter books.

The banded sea krait gets its name from its distinct coloring.

Elapids

Elapids are venomous snakes that include some of the world's deadliest, such as the cobra and taipan. These snakes are generally thin and fast-moving, with short **fangs** that are fixed in position at the front of the mouth. There are about 300 species of elapids. They are found in many regions around the world, especially in jungles. Coral snakes make up nearly a third of all types of elapids. Coral snakes are brightly colored, with bands of red, yellow, and black down the body. Sea snakes and sea kraits are elapids that live in water. They are almost as numerous as cobras.

◄ When the black mamba is ready to strike, it makes a threat posture by raising its head and front body 3 to 4 feet (1 to 1.2 meters) off the ground.

Vipers

All vipers are venomous. The family includes adders, rattlesnakes, and pitless vipers. Most vipers have a short, stocky body with a triangular head, and their **scales** are rough to the touch. Their long, hollow fangs fold back into the mouth. Many vipers have excellent **camouflage**. They blend with dead leaves and soil on the ground, so they are difficult to spot. Vipers are found farther north and south than many other types of snake. They are also found higher up in the mountains. One well-known viper is the rattlesnake of North America. The rattlesnake is easily identified by the rattle at the end of its tail. When it sheds its skin, old scales remain at the end of the tail. The rattlesnake will shake its tail as a warning before it bites.

▲ *Rattlesnakes are native to the Americas.*

▼ *A death adder may look like a viper, but it's really an elapid.*

Unlike other elapids, the death adder in Australia has fangs that fold back against the roof of its mouth, like a viper.

Worldwide Snakes

Most snakes are found in the warm parts of the world, especially jungles and deserts. But they are also found in **temperate** zones, and a few live as far north as the Arctic.

The yellow eyelash viper hides fangs in its upper jaw.

Jungle snakes

Snakes are most numerous and varied in the jungles of the world, where they are found living in the trees and on the ground. Many tree snakes are green and brown in color, perfect camouflage for living in the trees. Others are brightly colored and stand out from the green surroundings as a warning to other animals to stay away.

Hot and cold

Snakes control their body temperature by behavior. They can move into and out of the sun to control their temperature. When they are cold, for example, on cool spring mornings, they bask in the sun and absorb the sun's heat. When their body reaches the right temperature, they slither into the shade.

▶ Garter snakes are widespread. They have adapted to even extreme weather conditions.

Temperature control

The European viper is unusual as it can be found in more northerly regions, where the climate is cold in winter. It can survive the extreme winter cold by **hibernating**. It slips into caves and holes, where it remains in a deep sleep, allowing its body temperature to fall. In spring, the temperatures warm up, and the snake becomes active again.

◀ The puff adder and other snakes are often seen basking in the morning sun.

Snakes Adapt

Like other creatures, snakes have adapted to where they live. In some cases, they have changed their behavior in order to survive. In other cases, their bodies have changed over time.

▼ *Over time, the eyelids of snakes changed into see-through eye covers, which protect the eye from sand and the like.*

Extreme heat

Hot deserts can cause many problems for snakes, as the temperatures can be too high for them. Desert snakes slither into holes and caves, where it is cooler, and stay there until the temperatures fall. This is called **estivation** (es-tah-VAY-shun).

◄ *Black swamp snakes feed on frogs, tadpoles, and small fish.*

Water snakes

Sea snakes are found in the warm waters of the world, especially on coral reefs. Sea kraits are found on land and in water. They may look like other snakes, but true sea snakes live their entire lives in water. Their bodies and tails are flattened to create a paddle. This shape is perfect for swimming, but not for movement on land. Snakes do not have gills like fish. A snake has lungs, so it needs to come to the surface to breathe through its nose. Flaps help keep water out of the nose while they swim. A tiny amount of oxygen enters sea snakes through their skin.

▼ *The banded sea krait hunts in water but goes ashore to digest its meal.*

Sea snakes grow new skin every two to six weeks, which is faster than land snakes. This is because organisms in the water, such as algae, quickly cover the skin.

Life Cycle

Most snakes lay eggs in the ground. However, a few snakes give birth to live young.

Egg layers

Snakes produce eggs with soft, leathery shells, which are not as hard as bird eggs. Some female snakes make a shallow hole in the ground in which to lay their eggs. Others lay their eggs under rotting leaves.

In general, small snakes lay just a few eggs, and larger species lay larger numbers. A large python, such as the Burmese or reticulated python, lays up to 100 eggs. In the warmer parts of the world, female snakes may lay several clutches of eggs each year, but in the cooler regions they lay one clutch, sometimes doing so only every two to three years.

Parental care

Most snakes lay their eggs somewhere safe and leave them, but a few snake species stay to care for their eggs. Python eggs tend to stick together, making it easier for the female to surround and protect them. Certain pythons, such as the Burmese python, keep the eggs warm, too. The females keep the temperature high by moving their muscles, a bit like shivering, to release heat. This behavior is called **brooding**. Sometimes, the female leaves the clutch to warm up in the sun before returning to the eggs. The care she takes means more eggs hatch than if they were left in the ground. After the young wriggle out of the eggs, they are left to look after themselves.

▼ *When the eggs are being warmed, the female python usually does not eat anything.*

▲ *The tri-color hognose usually takes about 60 days to hatch.*

Nest building

The female king cobra is the only type of snake known to build a nest in which to lay her eggs. She scoops up leaves and twigs into a pile. Then, she lays a clutch of up to 40 eggs in the middle. She covers the eggs with more leaves and rests on top to guard the eggs from would-be predators, such as lizards and mongooses. When the eggs are about to hatch, her job is over and she slips away.

Hatching

Most snake eggs take two to three months to hatch. The baby snakes escape from their eggs by using a special egg tooth. It rips a slit in the shell that the baby snake can squeeze through.

Live birth

Some snakes, such as the adder, give birth to live young. The female holds her eggs within her body, and the young hatch inside. Then, the youngsters wiggle out of her body. Most of these snakes live in cooler parts of the world, where the ground is too cold for the eggs to develop. The young are kept warm inside the female's body.

Lifespan

Small snakes, such as the coral snake, may live for only five years, while larger snakes, such as pythons, can live for more than 40 years.

▼ *European adders can give birth to 20 live young at one time.*

Growing Up

Snakes grow very quickly when they are young. Although their growth slows down as they get older, they never stop growing. This means that the largest snakes are usually the oldest snakes.

New skin

A snake's scaly skin is tough. It provides good protection, but it does not stretch. The scales get worn from rubbing on the ground, so a snake replaces its old skin with a new one. This is called **molting**. When a snake is ready to molt, the old skin becomes loose. The snake rubs against a rough surface, and a break appears behind the snake's head. The snake wriggles out of its old skin, revealing fresh new skin underneath. Snakes molt every few weeks while they are young and growing quickly. However, as they get older they molt less regularly.

▲ The scales on a grass snake's back are shaped much like diamonds.

◀ When snakes molt, the clear scales over the eyes pop off with the rest of the skin.

Signs of molting

People can tell if a snake is about to molt. The first sign is the **opaque** eyes. Snakes have no eyelids, so a single large scale covers and protects the eye. When snakes are about to molt, the scale lifts a bit, giving the eye a milky appearance. The skin looks dull, and the snake stops feeding.

◄ *The molted skin is often left behind in one piece.*

Rattle

The rattle at the end of the rattlesnake's tail is formed from scales. When the snake molts, one large scale is left behind. This becomes dry, like a dried-up leaf. Each molt adds another scale, so the rattle gets longer.

▼ *The rattle is easily broken, so old rattlesnakes can have short rattles.*

Slithering and Sliding

Unlike lizards and other reptiles, snakes are legless. Because of this, they have other ways of moving around.

▶ A snake's smooth body allows it to slide over surfaces.

Snake skeletons

The snake's skeleton is very different from other reptiles. Its backbone is long and made up of as many as 500 bones, called **vertebrae**. These vertebrae are loosely linked together, so the snake can twist and bend its body. It also has many ribs and muscles. Humans and other **mammals** have a **breastbone** running down the front of the chest, but snakes don't. This allows snakes to wiggle and slither.

Snakes can slither across the ground at speeds of up to 12 mph (19 kph), but only for short distances.

◀ To move forward, most snakes throw their bodies in a series of curves and use their bellies to push against objects on the ground.

▶ *Sidewinders leave a characteristic "footprint" on the sand.*

Forward

Some snakes move in a straight line. They grip the ground with large scales on their underside and push their bodies forward. This is a slow way of getting around. It is used by larger snakes, such as pythons.

Side-to-side

Most snakes use a side-to-side, or wavelike, movement to slide forward. They push sideways against stones and other objects on the ground.

Sidewinders

Some desert snakes have found ways of coping with the hot, shifting sand. First, they lift the head and part of the body off the ground and throw that weight sideways. When the thrown parts touch the ground, the rest of the body moves in the same direction.

Climb, Glide, and Swim

Climbing snakes are adapted to life in trees, as are winged snakes. Though all snakes can swim, sea snakes make water their main home.

In the trees

The body of a climbing snake tends to be flattened. This allows the snake to hold its body rigid when reaching out to a branch. To climb, the snake grips the tree with its tail and reaches forward with its head. Once it has a grip on the next branch, the snake lets its tail go and moves upward.

Gliding snakes are found in the jungles of South and Southeast Asia. These tree-living snakes flatten their bodies from top to bottom to create "wings." They throw themselves off branches, flatten their bodies, and wiggle from side to side, as if on land. This gliding movement has been nicknamed "air-slithering." These snakes can travel more than 328 feet (100 meters) when they launch from the tops of tall trees.

▲ *Most tree snakes are the color of vegetation.*

▼ *The paradise tree snake is among the smaller of the gliding snakes.*

Under the water

Sea snakes use a side-to-side movement to go forward in the water, as land snakes do on the ground. The paddlelike tail pushes the body quickly through the water.

Sea snakes tend to prefer shallow, warm water. Though they cannot breathe underwater, they are capable of holding their breath for several hours.

▶ *A banded sea krait reaches the surface to take air into its lungs.*

Sometimes, eels are mistaken for sea snakes. The creatures look similar, but eels are a kind of fish. They have gills that allow them to breathe underwater. Sea snakes are reptiles with lungs.

Seeing and Hearing

Snakes use their excellent senses to find their prey. Their eyesight is not strong, but snakes have a keen ability to detect **vibrations** in the ground.

Eyesight

Many snakes have poor sight, so they rely on their other senses, but hunting snakes use their eyes to track prey. Often they stick their heads up above the ground to have a look around. Their eyes are very good at detecting movement, but not as good at seeing objects that are still. This means if a prey animal remains perfectly still, it may not be spotted by a snake.

▼ Green tree pythons spend much of the day coiled on branches. They can hunt at night because they do not rely on their eyesight.

▲ A snake places its jaw on the sand's surface, listening for movement. When the snake senses prey, it prepares to strike.

Day and night

Snakes that are active during the day tend to have round eyes with round **pupils**. Some tree snakes have horizontal pupils. This gives them good all-around vision to judge distances. Nocturnal snakes are active at night. Their eyes have to be sensitive in poor light. When these nighttime snakes are seen in daylight, their pupils become tiny slits. This prevents too much light from entering and damaging the eyes.

Hearing

Snakes do not have earflaps as people do. Instead, a snake's ear is hidden inside the head. Snakes have good hearing, and they can detect vibrations in the ground, too. When a person approaches, a snake detects the vibrations made by the feet, long before it can see the person. It can be dangerous to surprise a snake, so stamping the ground is a good way for people to alert snakes to their presence. When warned, snakes can slither away before people get close.

Other Senses

A snake's sense of smell is by far its most important sense. A snake has two small nostrils near the mouth. However, a snake mostly relies on its tongue for smelling.

The message

The snake flicks its tongue in and out many times a minute. It can even do this when the mouth is shut, because there is a small gap at the front of the mouth for the tongue. The tongue picks up scent particles in the air. It rubs the particles onto the roof of its mouth at a point called the **Jacobson's organ**. This organ identifies the scents and sends a message to the snake's brain.

Forked tongue

Why do snakes have a forked tongue? Both tips of the tongue pick up scents, and the Jacobson's organ can tell if there are any differences between the scents. If one tip picks up a stronger smell than the other, the snake will be able to determine from which direction the scent is coming. This helps the snake track its prey.

◀ *The forked tongue tastes the air to detect prey.*

Body heat

Pit vipers hunt at night, and they have the amazing ability to detect the body heat of their prey. They have special heat-sensitive organs on their head, between the eyes. These organs are so sensitive that the snake can detect tiny changes in temperature, as well as the exact position of the object producing the heat. This enables the creatures to hunt and attack prey in the dark.

Differences

The pit viper's ability to feel even tiny changes in temperature is sometimes called a sixth sense. Its special adaptations for smelling and detecting vibrations make it unique among animals. Mammals, such as humans, rely much more on sight and hearing.

Catching Prey

Snakes are expert hunters and have smart ways of catching their prey. Some lie in wait and ambush passing prey, while others give chase.

◀ *A grass snake stays alert to passing prey with the help of its tongue.*

▼ *The coloring of a Gaboon viper allows it to remain well-hidden, awaiting its next meal.*

Giving chase

Some snakes actively hunt prey. They push their heads into small cracks to flush out any animal hiding inside. Then, they give chase. When smaller snakes spot their prey, they move quickly. The chasing snake has good eyesight with which to spot prey.

Ambush!

Many snakes are perfectly camouflaged. They blend in with their surroundings, allowing them to hide unseen, waiting for prey to pass close by. Then, they strike quickly, lunging forward to grab the animal.

▶ *An African rock python can swallow a creature as large as an impala.*

Death by squeezing

Boas and pythons are constricting snakes. This means they squeeze their prey. They catch an animal with their mouths and quickly wrap themselves around the prey and squeeze. Every time the animal breathes out, the snake squeezes a bit harder so the animal suffocates. Once the animal is dead, the snake swallows it whole.

Feeding Habits

Some snakes have unusual feeding habits. Hook-nosed snakes mainly eat spiders. Other snakes feed on bird eggs. They swallow the eggs and crack them with their ribs. There is even a snail-eating snake. It pushes its lower jaw into the shell of a snail to pull out the juicy body hidden inside.

Swallowed whole

Snakes do not chew their prey. Instead, they swallow the prey whole. They are able to do this because their lower jaw moves in special ways. That is, the jaw can unhinge to open really wide. Snakes have a mouthful of small, backward-pointing teeth, which make it difficult for the prey to escape.

▼ *The front part of a snake's lower jaw separates and spreads apart from the side. The jaw opens wider and wider to allow large prey to be eaten while the upper jaw holds on to the animal.*

▲ A snake's body can expand after swallowing a large animal because it doesn't have a breastbone.

Slow lives

Once swallowed, the body of the prey passes into the snake's stomach, where it is slowly **digested**. A snake's digestion works slowly compared with that of birds and mammals, so it does not have to eat as often. Some snakes eat once a week, while others eat once a month. It is believed that some snakes can survive as long as a year without eating.

▼ A banded watersnake can swallow a bullhead fish whole. The snake swallows the head first, while the fish is still alive.

Venomous Snakes

Venomous snakes make venom, or poison, to kill their prey, rather than killing them by suffocation.

Making venom

Venomous snakes tend to have a triangular head. The shape helps hold the large **glands** that produce the venom. These glands are found on the side of the head, just below the eyes. Venomous snakes have fangs, which are large teeth with a groove down the outside. When these snakes bite their prey, the venom runs down the groove into the wound. However, some snakes inject venom with their fangs.

▲ *When the African puff adder strikes, the fangs spring forward.*

Special saliva

Venom is a bit like **saliva**. It is made of a mix of substances called **enzymes**. Enzymes help digest food. In a snake's venom, the enzymes attack the body of the prey, causing harm. There are several different types of venom, each working in a different way. For example, **hemotoxic** (HEE-moh-tawk-sick) venom attacks the blood, causing internal bleeding. This type of venom is produced by snakes such as pit vipers and the boomslang. Coral snakes, mambas, and cobras produce a **neurotoxic** (NER-oh-tawk-sick) venom, which attacks the brain and nervous system. It stops breathing and muscle movement, including heartbeats.

Each year in India more than 80,000 people are bitten by venomous snakes, resulting in nearly 11,000 deaths.

▶ *The Russell's viper is not often seen during the day.*

Most deadly

The most deadly snake in the world is the inland taipan of Australia. The venom from a single bite is enough to kill 100 humans. Fortunately, this snake is found in remote places, so few people are bitten. One of the most dangerous snakes is the Russell's viper of Southeast Asia. This snake lives in grassland and farmland and often enters people's homes. It does not flee when disturbed, but it hisses and bites. This snake is often stepped on because it is camouflaged. Thousands of people die each year from its venomous bite.

▲ *The bite of the inland taipan is said to have enough venom to kill hundreds of thousands of mice.*

Spitting cobras

Spitting cobras can spit their venom over several feet (meters) into the eyes of an attacker. This doesn't kill the attacker or penetrate the attacker's skin. However, it temporarily blinds the enemy, so the snake can escape.

▼ *The spitting cobra squeezes the venom glands in its head, forcing out a jet of venom.*

In Danger

Many venomous snakes are brightly colored. This is a warning to other animals that they are dangerous.

Copy cats

Sometimes, harmless snakes copy these warning colors, so they look as if they are dangerous. For example, the venomous coral snakes are small snakes with bands of black, red, and yellow. They have the most poisonous venom of all the snakes in North America, even more poisonous than the rattlesnake. The king snake and milk snake look similar to a coral snake, but they are harmless.

▼ *The milk snake is not venomous, but it will bite if attacked. It's better to leave it alone.*

Anti-venom

Anti-venom injections are given if somebody is bitten by a snake. The anti-venom acts against the venom. It has to be used quickly before the venom has done too much damage. Some anti-venoms work against a number of different snake venoms, but others are suitable only against the venom of one type of snake.

Anti-venoms are made using actual snake venom. Many venomous snakes are kept in snake farms, where they are "milked" to get their venom. To milk a snake, it is held firmly over a small container with a thin **membrane** over the top. The snake is forced to bite through the membrane. The venom drips down the fangs into the container and is used to produce anti-venom. Only professionals should attempt to milk a snake.

▶ *Venom taken from a pit viper is used to make anti-venom against its bite.*

Venoms have been used in medical treatments. For example, an extract from cobra venom is given to patients to thin their blood.

The Future of Snakes

Every year, thousands of snakes are killed, even harmless ones, because people are scared of them. Many other snakes are killed for their skins, including many **endangered** snakes.

Skins for fashion

Snakeskin can be made into high quality leather used to make expensive bags and shoes. The skin of the python has smooth, large scales and is particularly popular.

▲ Snakeskin is used for a number of popular items but is often taken illegally.

▶ Snakes like the Orlov's viper are considered endangered.

Rarest snakes

Because of snake killings and the destruction of their homes, almost 50 snake species are considered to be endangered or critically endangered. These snakes are at risk of becoming extinct. These snakes include the leaf-scaled sea snake, the Cyprus water snake, the Orlov's viper, and the Roatan coral snake.

When forests are destroyed, such as this one in Uganda, it affects the snakes and other creatures that live there.

Destroying homes

Snake **habitats** are destroyed when forests are cleared for farmland, industry, roads, and homes. Many snakes don't like being disturbed by people and their pets, so the snakes move away. As a result, snakes are losing their habitats all around the world.

Ways to Help

There are many ways to help save snakes. One of the most important ways is education.

Conservation

When people learn that they do not have to be afraid of every snake, they are less likely to kill them. **Conservation** organizations go into schools and teach young people about snakes. Often, the conservationists take live snakes so people can touch and even handle them.

Saving jungles

Jungles are home to more types of snake than any other habitat. Snakes are an important part of the jungle community. If the snakes disappear, other animals may disappear, too. By protecting the remaining jungles, and planting new ones, the snakes can survive.

◀ *The mole snake is protected in South Africa by a special government act.*

Banning sales

Another way to protect snakes is to make it illegal to sell the skin of endangered snakes. CITES stands for Convention on International Trade in Endangered Species of Wild Fauna and Flora. This organization oversees international agreements that ban the sale of certain animal products. Many snakes are protected in this way.

Success story

The Antiguan racer is a small, harmless snake found on islands in the Caribbean. In 1995, it was the world's most endangered snake, with just 50 individuals left. It had been hunted by predators, such as rats and mongooses. Conservationists worked hard to get rid of the predators. Now, there are more than 500 of these snakes.

▼ *The most endangered snake is the Antiguan racer.*

▲ *According to the International Union for Conservation of Nature, the king cobra is now listed as vulnerable.*

Facts and Records

~ Green anacondas are giants of the snake world. They can grow more than 20 feet (6 meters) long. They can weigh up to 550 pounds (249 kilograms).

~ The largest snake to have lived is named *Titanoboa*. It weighed more than a ton (tonne) and stretched to 43 feet (13 meters) long. That's as long as a bus. This kind of snake lived in the jungles of South America about 60 million years ago.

~ Some snakes have very long fangs folded back into the mouth so the snakes do not bite themselves. If a fang is damaged or lost, the snake grows a new one.

~ Grass snakes escape from their predators by pretending to be dead. They roll onto their backs and open their mouths.

~ Milk snakes get their name from the myth that they suck milk from cows. This idea may come from the fact that milk snakes come into barns and farmyards to hunt rats and mice.

The scales of a snake are made from keratin. That's the same material that forms human nails.

In India alone, millions of whip snakes and water snakes have been killed for their skins. The result of killing all of these snakes has been a huge increase in the numbers of rats and mice, which were hunted by the snakes.

King snakes and milk snakes are often killed because people think they are coral snakes. To tell the difference between the venomous coral snake and the harmless milk snake, people remember this rhyme: Red on yellow, kill a fellow; Red on black, friend of Jack. Still, it's better to stay away from wild snakes of any kind.

North America's largest venomous snake is the eastern diamondback rattlesnake, which can grow to more than 7 feet (2 meters) in length.

The longest North American snake is the eastern indigo snake, which can reach almost 9 feet (2.7 meters) in length. The eastern indigo is not venomous but is on the endangered species list.

Glossary

anti-venom substance that works against the venom of a snake

breastbone long, narrow bone at the front of the chest

brooding sitting on eggs to keep them warm

camouflage coloring that allows an animal to blend with its surroundings so that it cannot be seen

conservation protecting and managing habitats and the animals and plants that live within them

digested broken into energy from a food source

dinosaur large reptile that roamed Earth hundreds of millions of years ago and is now extinct

endangered at risk of becoming extinct

enzyme a substance that speeds up chemical reactions in the body, especially those involved with food digestion

estivation period of inactivity during hot weather

fang the tooth of a snake that is used to grip its prey; in venomous snakes, venom flows through the fang into the body of the prey

gland an organ in the body that releases a particular substance; for example, the salivary glands in the mouth release saliva

habitat a particular place where an animal lives, such as a jungle

hemotoxic affects the heart and blood

hibernating in a state of deep sleep

Jacobson's organ sense organ located in the roof of the mouth of reptiles such as snakes

mammal a warm-blooded vertebrate with hair; the young get milk from the mother

membrane a very thin layer of tissue

molting shedding skin

neurotoxic attacks the nervous system

opaque cloudy; not letting light pass through

poisonous harmful; venomous

predator an animal that hunts others for food

prehensile part of the body, such as a tail, that can grasp as a hand does

pupil black disc or slit in the middle of the eye through which light passes to the back of the eye

reptile a type of animal that usually lays eggs and has scaly skin, four legs, and a tail; reptiles include alligators, turtles, and snakes

saliva liquid produced in the mouth to wet food; a kind of body fluid with enzymes

scale a flap growing from the outermost layer of the skin, which becomes hard and forms a protective, waterproof covering with other scales

species a particular type of animal, such as a rattlesnake

suffocate to smother; to prevent an animal from breathing

temperate an area or a climate that has seasons, with cold winters and warm summers

venom poisonous fluid

vertebra a small bone that forms part of the backbone; more than one of these bones together are called vertebrae

vertebrate an animal that has a backbone, including fish, amphibians, reptiles, birds, and mammals

vibration a to-and-fro movement; shaking

Index